100 marvelously maddening
things about cats

LAGOON BOOKS

100 MARVELOUSLY MADDENING things about CATS

Series Editor: **Lucy Dear** Written by: **Jane Purcell**

Illustration:

Page layout: **River Design Ltd** Cover design: **Linley Clode**

Published by: **LAGOON BOOKS**, PO BOX 311, KT2 5QW, UK.
PO BOX 990676, Boston, MA 02199,USA.

www.thelagoongroup.com

Printed in Hong Kong

ISBN: 1904797407

100 MARVELOUSLY MADDENING things about CATS

1

Cats have nine lives. Which they waste by sleeping through eight-and-a-half of them...

2

A mutilated mouse carcass is their idea of a present...

3

Cats hang out with witches...

4

Only a cat would show affection by sticking its claws into you...

5

Cat breath...

6

Leave a pile of newly ironed sheets for three seconds and they will be mysteriously covered in dirty paw prints...

7

It would be easier to teach a cat Japanese than persuade it to swallow a worming tablet...

8

A cat has fleas, worms, ticks, ringworm, fur balls and a bad attitude...

9

When did you last hear of a cat pining away for its owner? Exactly...

10

Cats always practice their Yoko Ono impersonations just as you're falling asleep...

11

If cats are supposed to retain the instincts of the wild, when did you last see a pride of lions hanging round the kitchen while their owner struggled to open a can of gazelle chunks in gravy?

12

Showcats have unbelievably stupid names like Champion Ophelia Furbucket III...

13

A crowd of drunken football supporters makes less noise than two amorous cats...

14

Even on the ground a cat seems to be looking down at you...

15

More people in the world are allergic to cats than to any other domesticated animal...

16

Cats are natural screen villains. Imagine Blofeld with a dog...

17

All cats are Hannibal Lecter to the bird population...

18

The fact that cats will stare at a wall for two hours has led to a ridiculous notion that they're 'mystical'. They're not. They're stupid...

19

That furry bottom that has so recently pooed in your shoes is now perched on the kitchen table...

20

Pedigree cats are even more inbred than most royal families...

21

The cat in *Alien* survives, despite doing nothing constructive whatsoever...

22

The reason why there are no Guide Cats for the Blind is that the only places the owner would be 'guided' would be through cat flaps, up trees and under cars...

23

Anti-social human behavior invariably has a feline origin; cattiness, sourpuss, etc...

24

A wet cat is more bad tempered than a shark with toothache...

25

Persian cats are flat-faced furballs on stumps...

26

You know for sure that the retreating, straight up tail with the kink at the top is the cat's way of giving you the finger...

27

Describing a cat as independent is a polite way of saying a cat doesn't give a stuff about anyone...

28

A visit from the vicar affords the perfect opportunity for the cat to park itself on the carpet and spring clean his nether regions...

29

A dog will chase off a burglar...

30

A cat's fart is silent but more deadly than nerve gas...

31

A cat sleeps even longer than a teenage boy does...

32

A cat will wait until you're carrying a tray of spitting meat from the oven before weaving seductively round your legs...

33

Nothing in the known universe smells as bad as essence of tom-cat...

34

The arrival of your stuffy aunt perfectly coincides with your cat conducting a sex show with next-door neighbor's tabby...

35

Cats bond with women, get all the attention and steal all the food. Which is a man's job...

36

Your cat looks at you with such lofty contempt, you wonder if he were a model in a former life...

37

The only useful function a Persian cat can fulfill is as a feather duster...

38

Take the trouble to provide a cozy nest for your cat and it will be ignored in favor of your new cashmere sweater...

39

No matter how obviously fat, a cat can always yowl piteously enough to convince some fool it's being starved...

40

A cat is meager with sharing his affections but all too generous when it comes to his fleas...

41

Tom-cats are always getting into fights. And they don't even have drink as an excuse!

42

Cat fanatics are deeply humorless.
The slightest anti-feline sentiment and they're threatening you with death or a year's subscription to *Cat Lovers' Magazine*.
Don't know which is worse...

43

A well-fed cat will still chew through garbage bags, thoughtfully scattering bones and rubbish. Why not just cut to the chase and send out an open invitation to the rat population?

44

Your reward for letting a cat sleep on your bed is to have claws and teeth sunk into your leg at 4am...

45

If the cat can't actually reach the bird feeder, it will sit directly under like a malevolent sentry...

46

Cats learn their fighting technique from drunken men. Two hours of yowling followed by two seconds of flailing before both parties run away...

47

A black cat crossing your path may or may not bestow luck, but it will sure as hell trip you up...

48

Even if your cat is on another continent, it'll still hear if you open your refrigerator door...

49

Dogs are noble. Cats just have good posture...

50

No matter that you've covered that leftover chicken in more layers than an Eskimo, the cat will find a way...

51

So what if stroking a cat lowers your blood pressure? It will only shoot sky high again when you catch the furry little monster having a poo over your prize-winning roses...

52

A cat will turn on the charm when your friends are round. Just like men really...

53

That 'cute' kitten that decides to practice rock climbing on your lace curtains...

54

Your cat goes missing and after calling yourself hoarse, and searching the neighborhood, you find him snoring in the shed...

55

Cat bells...

56

Hearing a woman you fancy gushing on about her cats is deeply off-putting for most men...

57

You can spot cat fanatics a mile off...

58

Cat food sticks to the bowl like glued gravel...

59

Catwoman. All she ever did was hide out in really obvious places like a disused cat food factory, and give Batman a hard time...

60

Cats pooing over your tomatoes will always manage to stay just out of reach of that hurled boot...

61

The average tom-cat spends its life scavenging for food, peeing wherever it feels like it and never paying kitten support. No wonder men look enviously at them...

62

If you happen to be a poor goldfish, the cat parks itself outside your tank like a whiskered King Kong...

63

Catnaps are supposed to be the solution to workplace stress. Oh sure, we'd all function better if we were snoozing for 18 hours out of 24...

64

A cat will do its ‘oh-god-help-me-I'm-a-poor-creature-stuck-in-a-tree’ routine, until the fire department arrives. It will then leap nimbly to the ground, making you look a complete fool...

65

The most passive cat will yowl like a torture victim in the veterinarian's waiting room. This sets off the others, deafening everyone and earning you several dirty looks...

66

A cat is like an 18th-century courtesan. In return for groveling and extravagant presents, you might get a smidgen of affection...

67

**A dog will pine and howl at your grave.
A cat will lift its leg on it...**

68

Lions. Kings of the jungle? Pah! They lie about all day, scratching their nether regions while waiting for the lionesses to bring back some 'ready meals'...

69

Having to grit your teeth when the furry little monster ladders your last pair of stockings...

70

Cats always want to sleep in the most annoying places...

71

They molt. Everywhere...

72

The veterinarian makes you feel guilty for Tiddles' ongoing flea problem. It's hardly your fault if the cat hangs out with low lifes...

73

They may be furry and sweet but nobody minds if you hate rabbits. But profess to disliking cats and it's seen as a major character flaw...

74

Your cat falls into a pile of something unspeakable and you have to bathe it. And your reward? Severe blood loss and a tetanus shot...

75

Switch off the hall light and a cat will decide to stretch out half way up the stairs, like a furry death trap...

76

The most slothful cat will turn into a mountaineer when faced with a newly decorated Christmas tree...

77

A cat would happily step over your dead body for a plate of rabbit chunks in gravy...

78

Cats bask in the sunshine all day, but they never get sunburn or premature wrinkles...

79

Even the porkiest of cats never get stuck in a tight corner because their whiskers are always wider than their overstuffed rear ends. Why can't humans evolve a few whiskers?

80

There are laws preventing dogs from going to the bathroom wherever they feel like it...

81

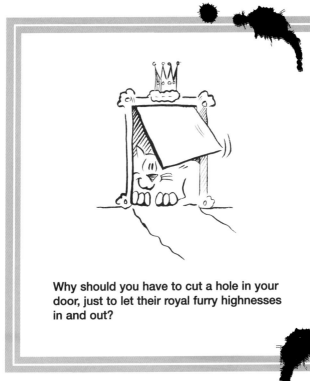

Why should you have to cut a hole in your door, just to let their royal furry highnesses in and out?

82

Cats are deaf to all orders and entreaties, except 'Would you like a great big plate of chicken?' Then they seem to understand every word perfectly...

83

You wake at night, sweating heavily, with a crushing tightness in your chest. Are you having a heart attack? No, monster cat is snoring on top of you...

84

They have scratchy tongues...

85

That no good feral tom-cat who's gone and
got your precious Siamese in the family way!

86

Cats could perform a genuinely useful function in winter, by lying down in front of the door and acting as feline draft excluders. Instead they find the warmest place in the house and refuse to move...

87

Because a cat can always sense when you are really annoyed with it, and it promptly reverts to 'kitten mode', wriggling about on the floor, looking supplicant and cute, so you stop being angry immediately. Instead, you are pathetically grateful for this tiny demonstration of affection...

88

If your dog refuses to enter a room, it might be haunted. A cat will happily curl up in a room occupied by the devil himself, so long as it's warm. In fact, the warmer the better!

89

Attempt to groom a cat and you will end up with more puncture wounds than a second-hand dartboard...

90

Animal trainers universally agree that cats are the hardest creatures to train...

91

You wake in the night to see two green lights glowing in the dark. Cats' eyes or alien death rays? Same difference...

92

The Ancient Egyptians thought cats were sacred, and most cats act like they still are...

93

Because, as Garrison Keillor said, 'Cats are intended to teach us that not everything in nature has a function'...

94

You take in a stray cat, shower it with love, bankrupt yourself with inoculations, and what does the ungrateful minx do? It decamps next door, just because they serve Deluxe Caviar Chunks...

95

Tom-cats are so uncouth...

96

Behind every collection of 'Best in Show' rosettes, is an exhausted owner and a cat that could not care less...

97

You buy a 100% Guaranteed to Drive Your Cat Wild catnip mouse and of course the cat ignores it. The only 'cat-nip' it's interested in is sinking his teeth into the postman's ankle...

98

Why should cats be the only animals allowed to go to the toilet inside the house...

99

Dogs can't be wrong...

100

No other animal has inspired such a plethora of ridiculous books...

LAGOON
BOOKS